My Country
Brazil

Annabel Savery

FRANKLIN WATTS
LONDON•SYDNEY

First published in paperback in 2013
by Franklin Watts

Copyright © Franklin Watts 2013

Franklin Watts
338 Euston Road
London NW1 3BH

Franklin Watts Australia
Level 17/207 Kent Street
Sydney, NSW 2000

All rights reserved

Dewey number: 981.066
ISBN: 978 1 4451 2703 3

Printed in China

Series Editor: Paul Rockett
Series Designer: Paul Cherrill
 for Basement68
Picture Researcher: Diana Morris

Franklin Watts is a division of
Hachette Children's Books,
an Hachette UK company.

www.hachette.co.uk

Picture credits: Atlaspix/Shutterstock: 4b; crazycoat/istockphoto:
20; Nicholas DeVore/Photoshot: front cover l, 12; Julio Etchart/
Alamy:17; Fabio Fersa/Shutterstock: 8; David R Frazier/Alamy:
14; Front Page/Shutterstock: 5; Ricardo Funari/Brazil Photos/
Alamy: 16; Robert Harding World Imagery/Getty Images: 15; Hemis/
Alamy: front cover c, 4t, 7 inset, 11 inset, 14 inset, 18 inset, 22;
Christopher Kolaczan/Shutterstock: front cover r, 13; Johnny Lye/
Shutterstock: 7; Edward Marques-Mortimer/Dreamstime: 18;
Paura/Dreamstime: 9; Picture Alliance/Photoshot: 10; Eduardo
Rivero/Shutterstock: 2, 21; Celso Sellmer/www.flickr.com/photos/
celsosellmer <http://www.flickr.com/photos/celsosellmer> : 19;
Spectral-Design/Shutterstock: 3, 6; Janine Weidel Photography/
Alamy: 1, 11.

Contents

All words in **bold**
appear in the
glossary on page 23.

Brazil in the world

My name is Natalia and I come from Brazil.

Brazil is in the **continent** of South America. It is the biggest country in South America, and the fifth largest in the world.

Brasília •

Rio de Janeiro •
São Paulo •

Brazil's place in the world.

I live in Brazil's **capital** city, Brasília. Brasília is a new city. Other cities, such as São Paulo and Rio de Janeiro, are much bigger and much older.

Brasília was built as a new capital city in 1960.

Brazil's landscape

Brazil has more than 7,000 kilometres of coastline.

Brazil is a huge country and has many different types of land. In the south there are high mountains and thick forests. On the east of Brazil there is a long coastline with lots of beaches.

In the north of Brazil is the enormous Amazon river.

The area around the Amazon river is made up of wet swamp lands and tropical rainforest. The weather here is hot and **humid**.

Millions of animals, insects and plants live and grow in the rainforest.

My favourite animal, the pink river dolphin, lives in the Amazon river. What's your favourite animal?

The weather in Brazil

The north of Brazil is near the **equator**. This means it is hot all year round. In the north-east there is not much rain, so there are often **droughts**.

The land gets very dry when it is hot and there is little rain.

In the south the weather changes throughout the year. It is coldest between May and September.

The warmer season is between October and April. This is also when it rains the most.

High up in the mountains it can get very cold, especially at night.

At home with my family

At home, I live with my mum, dad and my big brother Pedro.

Brazilians often have large families and live close together.

At weekends and holidays we go to visit our family in Rio de Janeiro and play games on the beach.

Rio de Janeiro is the second biggest city in Brazil. The biggest city is São Paulo.

Football is the most popular sport in Brazil.

I like playing football with my cousins. What is your favourite sport?

People who live in Brazil

Over time, many different people have come to live in Brazil. This means that Brazilian people today have **ancestors** from all over the world.

Brazilian people have European, African and Amerindian roots.

Most people live in the south where there are big cities. Towards the edge of the cities there are large **shanty towns**.

Other people live in the countryside, where they work on farms and raise animals.

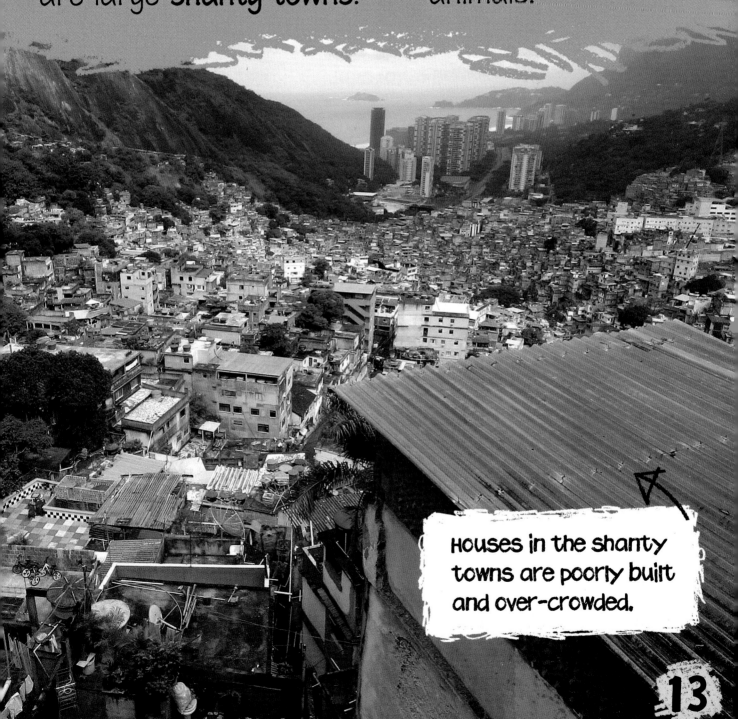

Houses in the shanty towns are poorly built and over-crowded.

What we eat

Most meals include meat, rice and vegetables.

The best thing about living in Brazil is the food. My mum is a great cook and at home we all eat together.

My favourite food is steak with black beans. What's yours?

Street stalls sell food that is ready to eat, such as *pasteles*. These are pastry envelopes with beef in the middle.

Brazil's national dish is *feijoda completa*, a meat stew with beans.

Feijoda completa is served with rice and slices of orange.

Going to school

Children in Brazil go to school from the age of seven to 14. I am still at primary school.

During the week I go to school for four hours every day, from seven in the morning until lunchtime.

My friends at school, studying hard.

Some children from poorer families do not go to school. They stay at home to help their parents, or go out to earn money.

This girl is making traditional crafts to sell.

Festivals and celebrations

Carnival is a huge celebration. It happens in February, before **Lent**, and lasts for five days.

In Rio de Janeiro the streets are filled with people in costumes, music and dancing.

Most people in Brazil are Roman Catholics. This means that we celebrate lots of religious holidays. In November we celebrate the Day of the Dead, when we remember people who have died.

People celebrate the Day of the Dead by lighting candles and taking flowers to relatives' graves.

19

Things to see

There are many amazing things to see in Brazil. Above Rio de Janeiro there is a big hill called Corvocado Peak. On top of this is an enormous statue of Christ the Redeemer.

The Christ the Redeemer statue is 38 metres tall!

For our last holiday we went to visit the Iguaçu Falls. This is a huge waterfall in the south of Brazil on the border with Argentina.

There are actually 270 separate falls. The drop is 60 metres high!

Here are some facts about my country!

Fast facts about Brazil

Capital city = Brasília
Population = 203,429,773
Currency = Real R$
Area = 8,514,877km2
Language = Portuguese
National holiday = 7 September (Independence Day)
Main religions = Roman Catholic, Protestant
Longest river = The Amazon (6,400km)
Highest point = Pico da Neblina (2,994m)

Glossary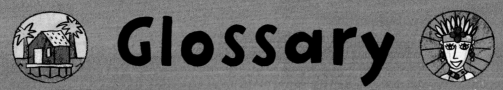

ancestor a person you are related to, who lived a long time ago

capital the most important city in a country

continent a very large area of land, there are seven on Earth

drought a long period of time when there is little or no rain

equator an invisible line that runs around the centre of the globe

humid having a lot of water vapour in the air

Lent the 40 days before Easter that Christians observe by fasting

shanty town a very poor area of a town that has poor quality housing

Websites

http://kids.nationalgeographic.com/kids/places/find/brazil/
The National Geographic Kids website has information and fun facts about Brazil.

www.brazil.org.uk/brazilintheschool/brazilforkids.html
A fun-filled site with lots of information about people and places in Brazil.

www.kidscornerbrazil.org/
Website designed for young learners with lots of information and links.

Books

Been There: Brazil by Annabel Savery (Franklin Watts, 2011)

Changing World: Brazil by Nicola Barber (Franklin Watts, 2010)

Countries Around the World: Brazil by Marion Morrison (Raintree, 2011)

Discover Countries: Brazil by Ed Parker (Wayland, 2010)

 Index